Where Did He Go?

To order additional copies of this book, contact:
Xlibris LLC
1-888-795-4274
www.Xlibris.com
Orders@Xlibris.com

This book has been put together
under the leadership and guidance
of the Holy Spirit. Love, prayer,
comfort and a need to
communicate with children
receiving and working with
computers at a young age.
Why not explain something that
must eventually happen to us all.

Where did He go?

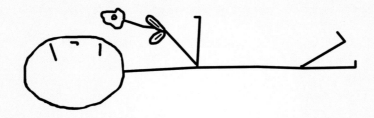

**Mommy * Daddy
Grandad * Grandmom
Uncle * Aunt
Brother * Sister * Cousin
Friend * Playmate * Classmate**

Special Thanks

One plants, one waters, but God
brings on the "increase"

To my Grandmother, Louise K. Hunt, who gave me
a wonderful mother and a beautiful name.

To my Family, my Sisters, Mildred, Carol and Teresa,
My Brothers, Leamond, Jr. and Kenneth
My Nieces, second to none and my Nephews, my Guys
Last but never least in my life, my Grandsons
Christian, Da'rhon, Kasheim, Hamza, And Eesa

To my Spiritual Sisters, who prayed with me at the
Unveiled Truth Ministries Prayer Retreat
at Blue Mountain.

And to my Spiritual Mother, Arizona Hart
who loves me **unconditionally**. Who thought it not robbery to
take me into her heart as a daughter.

CHERYLE SMALLS, Director
Spring Garden Day Care Center
Philadelphia Housing Authority

My Sister, My Friend
Your love for children became the wind
beneath the Wings of this Book and
taught it how to fly.

In loving memory of
Leamond Jackson
Sr., Louise K. Hunt,
Leamond Jackson,
Jr., and William "Will"
Bumpess

Dedication

To the memory of my mother,
Thelma V. Jackson
who left her 4 year old grandson, Jabari,
with unforgettable memories
and a question...

Where did she go?

To My Son, Jabari
My love for you is so strong that the Birth of
this Book has
been given life because of your love for a
Grandmother who
never left your heart.
You are My Diamond In The Rough.

Thelma V. Jackson

But of the tree of knowledge of good and evil, thou shalt not eat of it, for the day that thou eatest thereof thou shalt surely Die

Genesis 2:17

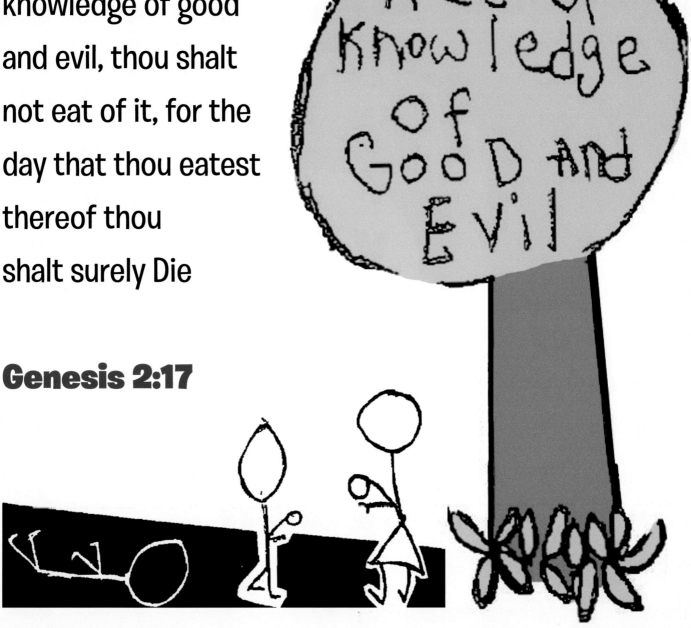

Who dies?

Young.

Old.

It is

Appointed

Unto man

Once to

Die...

Hebrews 9:27

Where has our loved one gone?
Heaven or Hell?

Behold all souls are mine;
But the soul that sinneth,
Shall surely die.

And I saw the dead, small and great,
Stand before God;
And the books were opened;
And another book was opened
Which is the Book of Life;
And the dead were judged every man
According to their works.
Revelation 20:12

And whosoever was not found
Written in the Book of Life
Was cast into the Lake of Fire.
Revelation 20:15

Will I ever see my loved one again?

You may see your loved ones in pictures,
memories, and good feelings.
Thinking good thoughts about them
help you see them in a different kind of way
that doesn't hurt.

But now he is dead
can I bring him back again?
I shall go to him,
but he shall not return to me.
II Samuel 12:23

If I cry will I still be a man?

Tears are natural emotions toward
joy and sorrow. Crying makes you
feel better from the inside out.
Crying washes away
the hurt...not
all at once, but
you feel better.

This is where a funeral takes place.

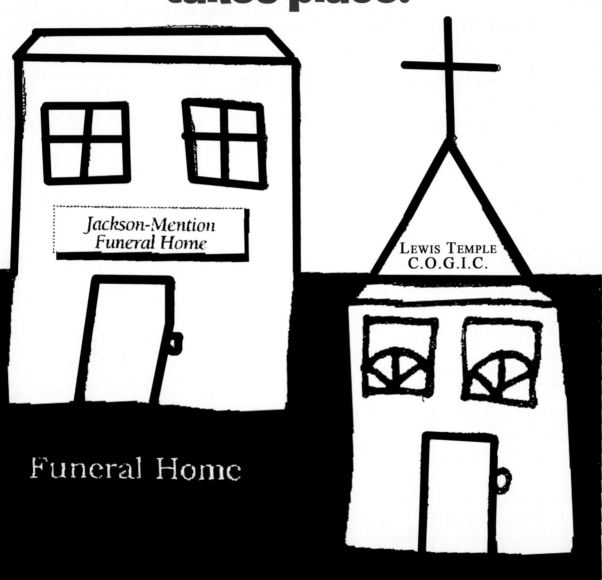

Funeral Home

Church

What comes next?

Funeral Home

Jackson-Mention
Funeral Home

Friends

Crying

What to expect there:

The coming together of family and friends at the Church or Funeral Home to physically see our loved ones.

A minister, who is also called a Preacher, will pray to God. He will pray that God will help everybody who hurts and feels bad about their loved one feel better and he will pray for those whose loved one who has gone to meet Jesus in judgement.

Friends

h h h h h h
h h h h h h
h h h h h h

Friends

ᴴ ᴴ ᴴ ᴴ ᴴ ᴴ
ᴴ ᴴ ᴴ ᴴ ᴴ ᴴ
ᴴ ᴴ ᴴ ᴴ ᴴ

Family

ᴴ ᴴ ᴴ ᴴ ᴴ ᴴ ᴴ ᴴ
ᴴ ᴴ ᴴ ᴴ ᴴ ᴴ ᴴ ᴴ
ᴴ ᴴ ᴴ ᴴ ᴴ ᴴ ᴴ ᴴ

What is a casket for?

To put people in the ground.
Putting them in a casket or, as it is
sometimes called, a coffin.

...Till thou return unto the ground...for dust
thou art, and unto dust thou shalt return.
Genesis 3:19

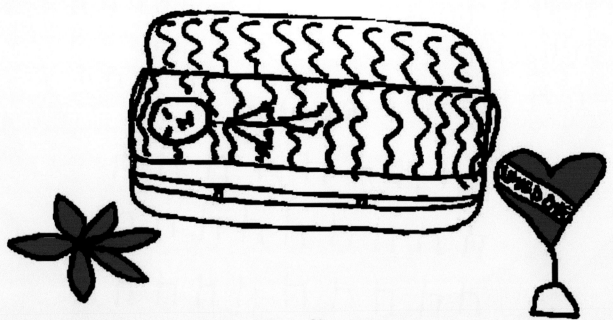

What is a cemetery?

A place where grass and a lot of ground are and our loved ones are put in a separate place with other people's loved ones.

Precious in the
Sight of the Lord
Is the death of
His Saints.

Psalm 116:15

23

Jabari and his grandmother

Mother and son

Printed in the United States
By Bookmasters